THE CONSTITUTION

The Constitution

by Brian Foley

Black Ocean
Boston - New York - Chicago

Black Ocean
P.O. Box 52030
Boston, MA 02205
blackocean.org

ISBN 978-1-939568-04-5

Library of Congress Cataloging-in-Publication Data

Foley, Brian, 1982-
[Poems. Selections]
The Constitution / Brian Foley.
pages cm
ISBN 978-1-939568-04-5 (alk. paper)
I. Title.
PS3606.O4228A6 2014
811'.6--dc23

2014000228

FIRST EDITION

TABLE OF CONTENTS

Self Assessment 3

I

The Constitution 7
Old Cold 8
Blown Out 9
Amendment 10
Object Lesson 11
Amendment 13

II

Covers 17
Here Does Nothing 18
Amendment 19
Moon Above the Law 20
A Panic Before the Rest 21
Amendment 23
Beauty Holds onto a Finger 24
"An Owe Stays Over . . ." 25
Enlightenment 26
To Gather Light 27

III

You Are On Fired 31
Amendment 34
Amendment 35
Complete 37
Suite 38
Free Radicals 40
Amendment 41
Rising 43

IV

Amendment 47
Here I Don't Come 48
Wrong Hammer 49
Cold Reading 50
Amendment 51
Gone Kite 52
Abandon 53
Amendment 54
The Birthdays 56
Extremities 59
Somewhere a Ceiling Clouds 60
Picador 61
Amendment 62
Changing Bulbs 64
Toothpick 66
Amendment 67

ACKNOWLEDGMENTS

Some of the poems from *The Constitution* originally appeared in one form or another in the following publications: *Action Yes*, *Anti-*, *Boston Review*, *Columbia: A Journal of Art and Literature*, *Dark Sky Magazine*, *Fou*, *Glitterpony*, *H_NGM_N*, *Horseless Review*, *ILK Journal*, *Poor Claudia*, the *Raleigh Quarterly*, *RealPoetik*, *Saltgrass*, *Softblow*, and *We Are So Happy To Know Something 2*.

Versions of these poems also appeared in the chapbooks *Going Attractions* (Greying Ghost Press, 2012), *The Constitution* (Horseless Press, 2011), and *The Black Eye* (Brave Men Press, 2010).

"You are on Fired" appeared as a pamphlet by Greying Ghost Press.

"To say many things is equal to having a home"
– Ezra Pound

". . . there is no revolt, it is the normal state"
– Wyndham Lewis

SELF ASSESSMENT

Already we need
hay to fill
our effigies.

The silence
of the heart
undermines

the body
which moves
in habit.

Put something
in it & leave

it to leaven.
It will rise like

the chimney
that stands

after the house.

I

THE CONSTITUTION

For the sake
of never regret
does differ deter
loss. Mostly we
soak. Shaped
by unattempt.

With you scrib-
bled beside me
I don't know
who I'm not.
Awareness is
just punishment.

I've not time
to humor a tree
compromising sky
to no end. Time
it takes. Take it
upon a self.

OLD COLD

We battlefields, gripped like
gargoyles perched on white buildings
panting, staring down our debt
invisibly fixed under the arm
like a deer tick.

It is an old cold, the sky blue as skin
holding everything out that would fall
in.

BLOWN OUT

Sun bites eye
shambles around

a corona
tightening a fist

the sky
wide with like

shaking me
a baby
in its mouth a wave

chasing away
sleeping horses I thought
I had traveled

far but concussion
depends on
how tall the grass is

AMENDMENT

Our first time
at dusk. Somehow.
We never scream.

In decision lives
a grenade. I guess,
blank with prey.

How much a stir
can slow understanding.

As soon as we finish
we want to be

understood again.

OBJECT LESSON

One wants to hire
the horrors of today

on the market
salt of
blood festivals
like a bankrupt
farmland

moaning home

more than
one angry Achilles
is made into

ideal values
drenched in heroics
finding nothing
but the hope worn

helmet
aesthetically

very approximate to
the experience of
battlefields

too bad
there are no longer such
unheroic heroes

too bad
my story will arrive
on the scene
with my corpse

all my strength
popped out

AMENDMENT

amazed at
the things I've taken

apart
lead without tracks

I'll die like light
I invent

I only feel
forget

to which I am
made

each of us
writes

the same world
over

the same world
separately

enough ant-
icipates you

believe fool
come free

II

COVERS

What you call cemetery doesn't bother me.
What does:
I can't help how an angel
lights a bed. Is an angel. How they gave themselves such word
"Angels."

No matter what
they will always be soft and barely, boats
that won't hitch
to the back of your throat.

HERE DOES NOTHING

I've asked a blank
piece of paper

to wishbone–words,
too quick to be rid of,

dream me back off.
It would not take gun-

point to fit me into
a simple question,

a chance more de-
finite than ever I was

worth, not knowing
gone came earlier.

AMENDMENT

some exits
enrage
eager to picture
the hurt

as a cicada
set high
in a cathedral

a mother
hovering over
a child

reach
bends us
but for what

creatured
by wait
and see

we eat reason
taste nothing

MOON ABOVE THE LAW

what we dress
slow

what erases it

we may
know

each

on our own companionship
what costs most

is no longer
not at fault

like the moon
things happen

only once in

A PANIC BEFORE THE REST

Eventually it isn't people.

You'll have fog, a dollar, clear sky
& then a cloud
interrupts everything apart.

If I wonder what genre is going to wake me
then, into tomorrow–

if it's the tire of the white
truck minding its own driveway of crushed
sea shells rolls out and wakes time

or the man
come down with himself is up
just to boil his water
back into place–

if all this that I hear from my bed is
the body alongside loneliness,

there is no way of knowing what will be
no way to say
wherever one never knows
all that is possible
but compares himself to anyway.

Just look in two eyes that years took out.

The talent of happiness,
words with no longer a strength
to guarantee & what I do not dream
these things are we.

AMENDMENT

what's felt addicts

even with eyes
loped

it's early enough
to be a few people

to deviate
more false than

the universe
exploding

a billion years
before we know it

I turn a dark
into an explosion

it seems impossible
I'm not hurt

BEAUTY HOLDS ONTO A FINGER

Grab this
finger a knife
almost pulled off—
It's still there!

You never drive
scared of accidents

I was once

an accident
a car come off
the road

demolishing the scenery
we insert our joke into
& I wouldn't have missed it

for the world
I never had

more fun than in
that hospital.

"AN OWE STAYS OVER . . ."

the warmth
you're not worth
collapsing into

a liquor
that lives longer
than love

conclusion-kiss
like an orphan fresh
after a bath

you'll not see
me fall down
in front of you

for the rest
of my life

ENLIGHTENMENT

Bang!
because life
wants us to.
if that were it

take money
and put it on
happy in pain.

Out of nothing
so much con-
fused with moons.

Erotic is our
shopping at rest
somehow loud

where night
is not thinking
us over.

TO GATHER LIGHT

it takes longer
to gather light
from under

to replenish
each please
thieved

over a gone
shoulder
put up with

what sea
could take it to the other
side

and bring
you to me to be
believed

where else
but in the frame love
forms

for the simple
reason
that it does not insist

III

YOU ARE ON FIRED

It's good you leaving
lulled like seaweed to the surface

Say goodbye to rock
responsible for the bone broke in all of us

Say goodbye to near sight bone
thick with invisible now certified by eye

See it nerve
as a sea without waves pantomimes
a release from movement

***

Say good to shame
acknowledge the cricket you hung
when it was too dark
has gone silent

Start your tenure
as a forest afraid to be petrified

Good stars you saw in sleep
live out their lives in no time

***

Dare to be good
breathing the air that will
one day inhale you

Good to erupt
into a soap bubble
thickening into wisdom
like a winter fur

& so surprised
I expect it

AMENDMENT

and then you remember
you've never eaten

discipline is like that
diminish, brute
to forgive

anything is acceptable
in hunger

a law lies down
like a dog
becomes breath

leaving home
constantly

AMENDMENT

Dusk buckets
some alive
feeling pulled

up from the all
day that
never dawned.

No longer
certain it is
the only

alternative
or even alter
native at all.

What you can
do without
can't grow.

Won't wither.
Won't crow.
Won't feed on

the dead.
But live
like live.

COMPLETE

where
a suddenly bursts
at a numbering length

it assumes
a room enters quietly
into itself

every body
talks about the weather but you

know
we can't choose our food
but we can eat

an excerpt
bigger than
a

SUITE

wedge
holding the door
open wide

I lodge
alone inside
what causes

love I
think of
a number

& cannot
imagine
a number

that big

what
I have for you
I have

trained to lie
still in my
hands

FREE RADICALS

in the former place

the sun stands

my calluses fall off
just an hour
from darkless

dumb impersonates calm
with a conversation feel

the eye that puckers
at mine

the eye half
my own fault

AMENDMENT

redacted black lines
as bored as I was

living kept
an infidelity
on purpose

how you never disappear
completely

allow yourself
a look

for shadows
good at surgery

& loneliness
a react to poison

to know
the difference

a privilege
I will not be a name

RISING

so teeth we can't touch
without dismantle but
we may taste shame
shared like a pet loved
against its will
pinched in exposed space
much too difficult for people
unable to halve their
own wilderness

IV

AMENDMENT

trouble is

resemblance
performs

an autopsy

pronounces me
out of body

then nothing
fits back in as it did
before it was

taken out

the bones I know
hunt for me
in someone else's rind

HERE I DON'T COME

a tremulous snow in my mouth

I turn my head
& cough back your shape
into the damp

unspoken
lack of place

purple as a splinter up
on your lip

to tongue the empty longitude
underneath the belly

singeing to fit

WRONG HAMMER

asked to
fetch the right
tool by my

father
incubated in

the wood under
sink under hood

***

in looking
through my chance

I walk into
the sea with clothes on

never find it
gets cold

COLD READING

it felt
like kidnap
a nub bank-
rupt

the way my bread
molted in the night

I need
a media
to kiss my
muscles

a mouse
I marvel before
the heart of
a palm

a few dried
crumbs settled
deep into the
cellar of a
lifeline

AMENDMENT

the rook
self conscious of
his side ways
climbs out of
the box
& moves
diagonally
knowing
gone is
his purpose

all's left
is direction
he exists
but without
a strike
is unable to
prove it

GONE KITE

the not yet
nearer than

the pause

turns far off

string
vulnerable
to test

distance
will disappear
the middle

of nowhere
has plenty
of lovers

ABANDON

it is difficult
to value what cannot
be named

the light of
a person

the world of that
feeling

a want to want without
residue

like a gashed onion
it demands a fee
let it be relief

a realm

AMENDMENT

I am under an impression

I stay alive
inside

attachments
instant

as the air is
previously owned

in buildings and streets
a deepening

resolve to stomach
the mistake in creation

provoked by presence
of revision

a wish
it wasn't obvious

I have woods
to finish

THE BIRTHDAYS

1.

children per-
forming parents
photo albums

reach
their image
& cease
existing

the door
off its hinges
carried away

with the
responsibility
of closing it

2.

when the frenzy of the wall
unwilling
to oscillate away

melts not
unlike any body
you've ever
stood inside

the space
between
fingers points
more than
their attachments

3.

the trees
oddly vacant
violent

with morality
to cede to
seasons greed

to clock
is not the job

where things
come from too
romantic for words

EXTREMITIES

fingeroil
takes

scales
off a fish

raincaked
& stitched

after flayed
& gulllicked

vent a law
for me
sliced thumb

leave your
belongings

in your mouth
mine

SOMEWHERE A CEILING CLOUDS

that eyes lap
when not looking

we know them later
to be quoting the waves

show me what ant
can open a vein

the lovely have
their own gauntlet

to run
our solutions

parachute & scissor
the string

while they must dance
to answer themselves

PICADOR

a red rag flows like rain in us
this suggested by course of black bull thorns
its charge conceals a hurt in the freedom of the howl

shadow invents
a sense of say nothing
every person becomes his own people

even the blush of the bluest dahlia will disappoint
you remember it
before it was rot

AMENDMENT

I’ve eaten too much I know
studying hunger

with whom I confuse
severally

I don’t want to move
through the rub-
ble of occur

the laid over tear
lasted on a
cheek

an in
exact face
a space for

shifting
weight against re-
pulsed cosmos

how many leaves
turn brown in my mouth

recurring down
the same
                    rust

like one too many

mornings
arrive leavings

to preserve
my indefinitely
made me

CHANGING LIGHTBULBS

Up all night
shuffling

pictures people
jumping

from tall buildings

the last
moment unwired

limbs could be
made bent

as a nail
on which nothing
can be hung

How I wish I could
whisper desperately to you

as if our lives
were about
to be extinguished

instead of floating

TOOTHPICK

No sign of the woodcutter

just a never ending
field of stump

seized in stocks
of chill blue earth
bare backs bent
like a knuckle

as if a king this way comes

picking his teeth
with their mothers

AMENDMENT

I remain unconvinced

these woods
are reversible

as a need
is no evidence
of absence

these are parasites
hidden in

every ear
every chicken heart
a tendency to keep
going round

we are very rarely
at the beginning
of something

if we are home
it is by accident

Warmth & Gratitude to Peter Gizzi, Dara Wier, James Tate, Jim Hoag & everyone at the UMass Program for their time & friendship. Love & respect to Anne Holmes, Arda Collins, Ben Estes, Ben Kopel, Caroline Cabrera, Carl Annarummo, Chelly Christle, Chris Deweese, Chris Sousa, Dan Chelotti, Emily Goodale, Emily Hunt, Emily Toder, Fra Chabrier, Gale Thompson, Heather Christle, Jack Christian, Jono Tosch, Josh Harmon, Julia Cohen, Leora Fridman, Lily Brown, Lily Ladewig, Luke Bloomfield, Mark Leidner, Mathias Svalina, Mike Young, Sarah Renee Marshall, Seth Landman & Wendy Xu. Love & tribute to my parents, Jim & Mary Lou Foley. Special thank you to Janaka Stucky, Carrie Olivia Adams & A. Minetta Gould for their care & confidence in this book.